QUICK & HEARTY MAIN DISHES

QUICK HEARTY & MAIN DISHES

Frank R. Blenn

 American Diabetes Association®

Publisher
Susan H. Lau

Editorial Director
Peter Banks

Managing Editor
Christine B. Welch

Associate Editor
Sherrye Landrum

Director of Production
Carolyn S. Segree

Printed in the United States of America
99 98 97 96 95   10 9 8 7 6 5 4 3 2 1

American Diabetes Association
1660 Duke Street
Alexandria, VA 22314

Page design and typesetting services by Insight Graphics, Inc.
Cover design by Wickham & Associates, Inc.

Library of Congress Cataloging-in-Publication Data

Blenn, Frank R., 1963-
Quick & hearty main dishes / Frank R. Blenn.
p. cm. — (Healthy selects)
Includes index.
ISBN 0-945448-46-5
1. Diabetes—Diet therapy—Recipes. 2. Entrées (Cookery)
I. Title. II. Title: Quick & hearty main dishes. III. Series.
RC662.B597 1995
641.5'6314—dc20   95-5679 CIP

CONTENTS

FOREWORD

The American Diabetes Association is proud to announce *Healthy Selects*, a new cookbook series dedicated to the premise that light, healthy food can be good for you *and* taste great, too. *Quick & Hearty Main Dishes*, the fourth book in the series, is a collection of easy-to-prepare main dish recipes you can serve at elegant parties or comfortable family dinners. Each recipe has American Diabetes Association–approved exchanges and all nutritional information provided. We know you'll enjoy the new ways to serve some of your favorite foods, as well as the unique ideas found in the series.

Author Frank Blenn created these recipes to help others cope with diabetes, and thought to offer them to us in an effort to reach and assist a wider audience. We deeply appreciate his generosity. The Association owes a special debt of gratitude to Madelyn L. Wheeler, MS, RD, CDE, and her company, Nutritional Computing Concepts, for the thorough and careful preparation of nutritional calculations and exchange information. Ms. Wheeler offered many valuable suggestions through each step of the book production process. Robyn Webb Associates conducted taste-testing on every recipe and ensured the accuracy and quality of the finished product. Ms. Webb also developed many of the recipes in this book.

The original manuscript was reviewed by Karmeen Kulkarni, MS, RD, CDE, and Madelyn Wheeler, MS, RD, CDE. The final manuscript was reviewed by Sue McLaughlin, RD, CDE, and David B. Kelley, MD. Patty Walsh provided creative illustrations for each title in the series.

Have fun adding variety and zest to your diet with the *Healthy Selects* Series!

American Diabetes Association

PREFACE

Quick & Hearty Main Dishes is the fourth cookbook in a new series offering lighter and healthier recipes that still taste wonderful. I served many of these recipes, with great success, at elegant parties and casual dinners. I know you will appreciate the abundance of ways to serve the delicious recipes presented in this series.

My long-term goal was to write and share the results with you. With that in mind, I would like to offer my warmest and most sincere appreciation to the American Diabetes Association in helping me reach my goal. Without their interest and assistance, this series of books would just be another manuscript in my office.

I would like to dedicate this book to my family, who encouraged me to find a wider audience, and to my close friends (who are never without their opinions!) for taste-testing their way through many joyful times.

I hope you enjoy these delicious additions to a varied and healthy diet.

Frank R. Blenn

INTRODUCTION

Packed with tasty and easy-to-prepare recipes for main dishes, *Quick & Hearty Main Dishes* is a terrific addition to your cookbook library. There are some important points to keep in mind, however, as you try all the recipes:

◆ The nutrient analysis section *only includes* the ingredients listed in the ingredients section! The nutrient analyses do *not* include serving suggestions sometimes provided in other sections of the recipe. For example, in the recipe for Broiled Salmon Steaks, we suggest that you serve them with a little nonfat sour cream or plain yogurt flavored with spices. But, because neither sour cream nor yogurt is included as an ingredient, you know that the nutrient analysis only applies to the Broiled Salmon Steaks recipe itself. Similarly, suggested garnishes are not included in the analyses, unless they appear in the ingredients list.

◆ In general, we have suggested using olive oil instead of low-calorie margarine. You can use low-calorie margarine if you prefer, depending on your individual goals. Olive oil provides more monounsaturated fats, which are healthier, but low-calorie margarine does contain fewer calories. Feel free to interchange them if you need to.

◆ If you can find a version of an ingredient lower in fat than the low-fat items we used, feel free to use it instead. The recipes will still work, and your total fat grams will go down slightly. We usually use low-fat options, defined as containing 3 grams of fat or less per serving. When we use the term *low calorie*, that means 40 calories or less per serving. Lite soy sauce is lower in sodium than regular soy sauce. When we say a dash of salt, that's 1/16 of a teaspoon.

◆ In terms of nutrient values, 1 Starch/Bread Exchange can be interchanged with 1 Fruit Exchange.

◆ Note that the serving sizes in these recipes are not uniform, and vary from recipe to recipe.

Good luck, and we hope you enjoy *Quick & Hearty Main Dishes*.

ANY DAY PASTA

MAKING PERFECT PASTA

There are at least 150 varieties of pasta to choose from; with the right sauce, pasta is a healthy, low-fat food. Pasta has only about 210 calories per cooked cup and is a good source of complex carbohydrates and B vitamins. Here are a few tips to insure perfect pasta-making all the time.

♦ To cook pasta, start by bringing a cold pot of water to a full rolling boil; this ensures that the pasta cooks properly. Cook pasta to the al dente stage: tender, but still slightly chewy.

♦ Rinse the pasta with cool water to remove the surface starch if you desire, but the starch that clings to the pasta actually helps sauces adhere better.

♦ Cooked pasta lasts for a week in the refrigerator if placed in a covered container; dry pasta in the box will last in your cupboard for a year. Do not freeze cooked pasta, except in casseroles like lasagna.

CORKSCREW PASTA WITH SAGE AND PEPPERS

8 servings/serving size: 1 cup

A very simple dish that looks so pretty.

- 2 Tbsp. chicken broth
- 1 garlic clove, minced
- 1/2 cup chopped onion
- 1/2 each red, green, and yellow peppers, cut into thin strips
- 2 Tbsp. chopped fresh sage
- 15 oz. tomato puree
- 1 Tbsp. tomato paste
- 2 Tbsp. red wine
- 1 tsp. crushed red pepper (optional)
- 1 lb. cooked corkscrew pasta (or any other shaped pasta)

1. In a large skillet over medium heat, heat broth. Add garlic and onion, and saute for 5 to 8 minutes. Add peppers, and saute for another 7 minutes.
2. Add sage, tomato puree, tomato paste, red wine, and red pepper. Lower heat to a simmer, and cook for 15 minutes.
3. Add cooked pasta, and let stand for 5 minutes. Serve.

••

Starch/Bread Exchange 1	Cholesterol .... 0 milligrams
Vegetable Exchange 1	Total Carbohydrate .... 24 grams
Calories 115	Dietary Fiber .... 1 gram
Total Fat .... 1 gram	Sugars .... 4 grams
Saturated Fat .... 0 grams	Protein .... 4 grams
Calories from Fat 5	Sodium .... 231 milligrams

EGGPLANT LASAGNA*

6 servings/serving size: about 1 cup

*L*ayers of tender eggplant replace noodles in this hearty entree that can be made ahead and frozen.

- Nonstick cooking spray
- 1-3/4 cup chopped onion
- 2 medium garlic cloves, minced
- 16 oz. whole tomatoes, undrained
- 1/4 cup tomato paste
- 2 Tbsp. fresh chopped parsley
- 1 tsp. oregano
- 1/2 tsp. dried basil
- Fresh ground pepper
- 1 large eggplant, peeled and sliced into 1/4-inch slices
- 1 cup shredded skim-milk mozzarella cheese
- 1 cup low-fat cottage cheese
- 4 Tbsp. grated Parmesan cheese

1. Coat a large skillet with nonstick cooking spray. Add onion and garlic, and saute over low heat until onion is tender, about 6 minutes.
2. Stir in undrained whole tomatoes, tomato paste, parsley, salt, oregano, basil, and pepper. Bring mixture to a boil. Reduce heat and simmer, uncovered, for 40 to 50 minutes, stirring occasionally.
3. To steam eggplant slices, place 1 inch of water in a large pot. Arrange eggplant slices on a steamer, cover pot, and steam until eggplant is tender, about 5 minutes. Do not overcook.
4. Combine mozzarella and cottage cheeses together and set aside.
5. Coat a 13x9x2-inch baking pan with cooking spray, and place half of the eggplant in the pan. Top eggplant with half of the sauce mixture and half of the cheese mixture, and sprinkle with Parmesan cheese. Repeat the steps in layers until all the ingredients are used.
6. Bake at 350 degrees for 30 to 35 minutes, and serve hot.

....

Starch/Bread Exchange	1	Cholesterol	19 milligrams
Medium-Fat Meat Exchange	1	Total Carbohydrate	18 grams
Vegetable Exchange	1	Dietary Fiber	3 grams
Calories	177	Sugars	11 grams
Total Fat	6 grams	Protein	15 grams
Saturated Fat	4 grams	Sodium	546 milligrams
Calories from Fat	54		

* This recipe is relatively high in sodium.

GREEN PASTA WITH TOMATO SAUCE

2 servings/serving size: about 1 cup

You probably have these ingredients in your cupboard right now.

- 1/4 lb. uncooked spinach fettucine
- 2/3 cup skim milk ricotta cheese
- 1/2 cup canned tomatoes
- 1 large garlic clove, minced
- 1 small onion, finely chopped
- 1/4 tsp. dried oregano
- 1/2 tsp. dried basil
- 1 Tbsp. grated Parmesan cheese

1. Prepare the pasta according to package directions, drain, and rinse thoroughly.
2. Place the pasta in a 1-qt. casserole dish, and spoon ricotta cheese in center of pasta. Cover and bake at 300 degrees for 8 to 10 minutes until ricotta is heated through.
3. In a small saucepan, combine the tomatoes with the remaining ingredients, bring to a boil, reduce the heat, and let simmer for 3 to 5 minutes or until onion is tender.
4. Remove pasta from oven, and spoon sauce around ricotta cheese. Sprinkle Parmesan cheese over all and serve.

....

Medium-Fat Meat Exchange 1	Cholesterol .... 82 milligrams
Starch/Bread Exchange 3	Total Carbohydrate .... 53 grams
Vegetable Exchange 1	Dietary Fiber .... 5 grams
Fat Exchange 1	Sugars .... 12 grams
Calories 382	Protein .... 20 grams
Total Fat .... 10 grams	Sodium .... 292 milligrams
Saturated Fat .... 5 grams	
Calories from Fat 91	

BAKED MACARONI AND CHEESE

6 servings/serving size: 1 cup

*C*reamy smooth and oh so comforting.

- 1 cup uncooked elbow macaroni
- 2 egg substitute equivalents
- 1 cup evaporated skim milk
- 1 cup small curd low-fat cottage cheese
- 1/4 cup shredded sharp cheddar cheese

- Dash salt
- Fresh ground pepper
- 1 Tbsp. Dijon mustard
- Nonstick cooking spray
- 1 Tbsp. fine dried bread crumbs (to further reduce sodium, see recipe, page 26, for homemade version)

1. Prepare macaroni according to package directions, omitting salt. Drain and set aside.
2. In a large mixing bowl, combine the remaining ingredients except the bread crumbs with the cooked macaroni.
3. Coat a 1-qt. baking dish with cooking spray and spoon the mixture into the dish. Sprinkle the top with bread crumbs. Bake at 350 degrees for 1 hour and serve hot.

Starch/Bread Exchange 1-1/2
Lean Meat Exchange 1
Calories 170
Total Fat .... 3 grams
  Saturated Fat .... 2 grams
  Calories from Fat 26
Cholesterol .... 10 milligrams
Total Carbohydrate .... 21 grams
  Dietary Fiber .... 0 grams
  Sugars .... 6 grams
Protein .... 14 grams
Sodium .... 324 milligrams

PASTA WITH CHICK PEAS AND GARLIC

8 servings/serving size: 1 cup

*T*he dish is a jumble of delicious Italian ingredients you probably already have on hand.

- 1 Tbsp. olive oil
- 3 garlic cloves, minced
- 1/2 cup minced onion
- 1/2 cup sliced carrots
- 1 cup chopped spinach or escarole, stems trimmed, washed, and dried
- 15 oz. chopped plum tomatoes, drained

- 1 tsp. chopped fresh rosemary
- 1 cup chick peas, drained and rinsed
- 1/4 cup minced fresh parsley
- 1 lb. cooked shells (or other shaped pasta)
- Fresh ground pepper

1. In a large skillet over medium heat, heat oil. Add garlic and onions, and saute for 5 minutes. Add carrots, and saute for 5 minutes more.
2. Add chopped spinach or escarole, tomatoes, rosemary, and chick peas, and simmer over low heat for 3 minutes. Sprinkle with parsley.
3. Toss cooked pasta with chick pea and tomato mixture. Add fresh ground pepper and toss well. Serve.

....

Starch/Bread Exchange 1-1/2	Cholesterol .... 0 milligrams
Vegetable Exchange 1	Total Carbohydrate .... 26 grams
Calories 147	Dietary Fiber .... 3 grams
Total Fat .... 3 grams	Sugars .... 4 grams
Saturated Fat .... 0 grams	Protein .... 5 grams
Calories from Fat 25	Sodium .... 102 milligrams

SPAGHETTI PIE

4 servings/serving size: approximately 1 cup

A *great way to use leftover spaghetti.*

- **4 cups cooked spaghetti (about 1/2 lb. dry)**
- **2 egg whites**
- **2 Tbsp. skim milk**
- **1/4 cup grated fresh Parmesan cheese**
- **1 tsp. dried oregano**
- **1 tsp. dried basil**
- **1 tsp. paprika**
- **1/2 tsp. rosemary**

1. In a medium bowl, combine all ingredients and mix well.
2. Pour spaghetti mixture into an ovenproof nonstick round casserole dish or skillet and spread evenly.
3. Bake pie, uncovered, at 350 degrees until golden brown, about 20 minutes. Cut into wedges and serve.

....

Starch/Bread Exchange 3
Calories 232
Total Fat .... 3 grams
   Saturated Fat .... 1 gram
   Calories from Fat 23
Cholesterol .... 4 milligrams

Total Carbohydrate .... 40 grams
   Dietary Fiber .... 2 grams
   Sugars .... 2 grams
Protein .... 11 grams
Sodium .... 126 milligrams

MARINARA SAUCE

20 servings/serving size: 1/4 cup

Keep a batch on hand in the freezer. The taste compliments shrimp or pasta and is a great dipping sauce for baked chicken fingers.

- ◆ **24 oz. tomato puree**
- ◆ **1 green pepper, chopped**
- ◆ **1/2 cup minced onion**
- ◆ **1 tsp. dried oregano**
- ◆ **1/2 lb. mushrooms, sliced**
- ◆ **1 red pepper, chopped**
- ◆ **1 tsp. dried basil**
- ◆ **1/2 tsp. garlic powder**

1. In a large saucepan over medium heat, combine all ingredients, mixing thoroughly. Let simmer 40 to 50 minutes, allowing flavors to blend.

Vegetable Exchange 1
Calories 19
Total Fat . . . . 0 grams
　Saturated Fat . . . . 0 grams
　Calories from Fat 0
Cholesterol . . . . 0 milligrams

Total Carbohydrate . . . . 5 grams
　Dietary Fiber . . . . 0 grams
　Sugars . . . . 2 grams
Protein . . . . 1 gram
Sodium . . . . 135 milligrams

STUFFED MANICOTTI*

4 servings/serving size: 2 stuffed manicotti

You can also use the filling for a lasagna or stuffed shells.

- 2 Tbsp. low-sodium chicken broth
- 1/2 cup minced onion
- 1/2 cup minced carrot
- 1 garlic clove, minced
- 1 cup low-fat ricotta cheese
- 1 egg substitute equivalent
- 2 Tbsp. fresh grated Parmesan cheese
- 1 Tbsp. chopped fresh basil
- 8 large manicotti shells, cooked
- 2 cups Marinara Sauce (see recipe, page 8)

1. In a skillet over medium heat, heat broth. Add onion, carrot, and garlic, and saute for 5 to 7 minutes, until onion is tender.
2. In a large bowl, combine vegetables with ricotta cheese, egg, Parmesan cheese, and basil. Mix well.
3. Stuff some of the mixture into each shell. Place stuffed manicotti shells in a large casserole dish. Pour Marinara Sauce on top, and let cook at 350 degrees for 20 minutes.

Starch/Bread Exchange 2-1/2
Lean Meat Exchange 1
Vegetable Exchange 1
Calories 275
Total Fat .... 4 grams
  Saturated Fat .... 2 grams
  Calories from Fat 34

Cholesterol .... 27 milligrams
Total Carbohydrate .... 45 grams
  Dietary Fiber .... 3 grams
  Sugars .... 8 grams
Protein .... 18 grams
Sodium .... 458 milligrams

* This recipe is relatively high in sodium.

VEGETABLE LO MEIN

8 servings/serving size: 1 cup

Restaurant style lo mein has far too much fat to be considered healthy, so make this lower-fat version instead.

- 1 cup plus 2 Tbsp. low-sodium chicken broth
- 2 garlic cloves, minced
- 1/4 cup minced scallions
- 2 tsp. grated fresh ginger
- 2 carrots, peeled and cut into 1/4-inch slices
- 3 celery stalks, cut on the diagonal into 1/4-inch slices
- 1/2 cup sliced mushrooms
- 1-1/2 cups broccoli florets
- 2 Tbsp. dry sherry
- 1 Tbsp. lite soy sauce
- 1 tsp. sesame oil
- 1 Tbsp. cornstarch
- 1/2 lb. cooked thin spaghetti noodles

1. In a large skillet or wok, heat 2 Tbsp. of broth. Add garlic, scallions, and ginger, and stir-fry for 30 seconds.
2. Add carrots, celery, and mushrooms, and stir-fry for 5 minutes. Add broccoli and 1/2 cup of broth, cover, and steam for 5 minutes.
3. In a small bowl, combine the remaining 1/2 cup of broth with sherry, soy sauce, and sesame oil. Add cornstarch and mix well.
4. Remove cover, and add cornstarch mixture. Cook for 1 minute more, until mixture thickens. Toss in cooked noodles and mix well. Serve.

....

Starch/Bread Exchange	1	Cholesterol	0 milligrams
Vegetable Exchange	1	Total Carbohydrate	17 grams
Calories	92	Dietary Fiber	3 grams
Total Fat	1 gram	Sugars	3 grams
Saturated Fat	0 grams	Protein	3 grams
Calories from Fat	11	Sodium	128 milligrams

BAKED LEMON CHICKEN

4 servings/serving size: 3 oz.

A very light chicken dish for a spring or summer night.

- ◆ **3 Tbsp. lemon juice**
- ◆ **1 tsp. fresh lemon zest**
- ◆ **1 Tbsp. finely chopped onion**
- ◆ **1/4 tsp. paprika**
- ◆ **2 Tbsp. olive oil**

- ◆ **Dash salt**
- ◆ **Fresh ground pepper**
- ◆ **2 whole boneless, skinless chicken breasts, halved**

1. In a small bowl, combine all ingredients except chicken.
2. Place chicken in a shallow baking dish and pour lemon mixture over it. Bake in a 400-degree oven for 45 minutes until chicken is tender. Transfer chicken to a serving platter, spoon juices over it, and serve.

Lean Meat Exchange	3	Cholesterol	72 milligrams
Fat Exchange	1/2	Total Carbohydrate	1 gram
Calories	205	Dietary Fiber	0 grams
Total Fat	10 grams	Sugars	0 grams
Saturated Fat	2 grams	Protein	27 grams
Calories from Fat	88	Sodium	100 milligrams

CHICKEN AND SHRIMP*

4 servings/serving size: 2–3 oz. chicken and shrimp combined plus rice

A skillet dinner that cooks nicely while you prepare a salad and crusty bread.

- 1 Tbsp. olive oil
- 2 medium onions, chopped
- 2 garlic cloves, minced
- 1 cup chopped celery
- 1 green pepper, chopped
- 2/3 cup uncooked rice
- 2 cups low-sodium chicken broth
- 1-1/2 cups cubed precooked chicken
- 16 oz. stewed tomatoes
- 4 oz. shrimp, shelled and deveined
- 1 tsp. hot pepper sauce
- Fresh ground pepper

1. Coat a large skillet with the oil and heat over medium heat. Add onion, garlic, celery, and green pepper; saute until tender.
2. Stir in the rice, broth, chicken, and tomatoes. Bring to a boil, reduce the heat, and let simmer for 25 minutes. Add the shrimp, hot pepper sauce, and pepper and let simmer for 5 minutes. Transfer to a serving platter to serve.

....

Lean Meat Exchange	2	Cholesterol	80 milligrams
Starch/Bread Exchange	2-1/2	Total Carbohydrate	43 grams
Vegetable Exchange	1	Dietary Fiber	3 grams
Calories	349	Sugars	13 grams
Total Fat	9 grams	Protein	25 grams
Saturated Fat	2 grams	Sodium	430 milligrams
Calories from Fat	79		

* This recipe is relatively high in sodium.

CHICKEN WITH WINE SAUCE

4 servings/serving size: 3 oz.

*C*hicken with a comforting creamlike sauce.

- ◆ 4 Tbsp. olive oil
- ◆ 2 whole boneless, skinless chicken breasts, halved
- ◆ 3 Tbsp. flour
- ◆ 1/2 cup low-sodium chicken broth
- ◆ 1 cup low-fat sour cream
- ◆ 3/4 cup white wine
- ◆ 1/2 tsp. lemon pepper
- ◆ 2 tsp. lemon rind
- ◆ 1/2 cup sliced mushrooms
- ◆ Parsley sprigs

1. Place 2 Tbsp. of oil in a shallow baking pan; place chicken breasts in oil and bake at 350 degrees for 15 minutes.
2. Place remaining 2 Tbsp. of oil and flour in a saucepan and blend well. Add broth and continue stirring until mixture is smooth. Add sour cream, wine, lemon rind, and lemon pepper. Stir until well blended.
3. Remove chicken from oven and turn. Cover with mushrooms and pour sauce on top. Continue baking uncovered for 20 minutes or until tender. Transfer to a platter and garnish with parsley.

....

Medium-Fat Meat Exchange 4	Cholesterol .... 72 milligrams
Starch/Bread Exchange 1	Total Carbohydrate .... 13 grams
Calories 378	Dietary Fiber .... 0 grams
Total Fat .... 21 grams	Sugars .... 8 grams
Saturated Fat .... 5 grams	Protein .... 32 grams
Calories from Fat 187	Sodium .... 151 milligrams

CHICKEN AND ZUCCHINI

8 servings/serving size: 3–4 oz.

A quick stir-fry dish with a hint of ginger.

- 1 Tbsp. olive oil
- 4 whole boneless, skinless chicken breasts, cut into thin strips about 1/8-inch wide
- 2 garlic cloves, minced
- 1 tsp. grated fresh ginger
- 1 Tbsp. lite soy sauce
- 1/3 cup sliced celery
- 1/2 cup sliced fresh mushrooms
- 1 cup julienned zucchini
- 2 tsp. cornstarch
- 3 Tbsp. water

1. Heat the oil in a large skillet or wok. Add the chicken, garlic, and ginger. Stir fry until chicken turns white, about 5 minutes. Stir in the soy sauce, celery, mushrooms, and zucchini.
2. Cover and continue to cook for about 5 minutes.
3. Add the cornstarch to the water and slowly add this mixture to the chicken, stirring constantly. Continue to cook for 2 to 5 minutes until mixture is thickened. Remove from heat and serve.

....

Lean Meat Exchange 3	Total Carbohydrate . . . . 2 grams
Calories 165	Dietary Fiber . . . . 0 grams
Total Fat . . . . 5 grams	Sugars . . . . 1 gram
Saturated Fat . . . . 1 gram	Protein . . . . 27 grams
Calories from Fat 43	Sodium . . . . 143 milligrams
Cholesterol . . . . 72 milligrams	

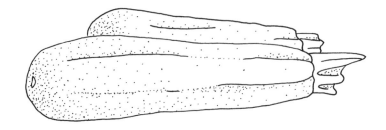

CHICKEN PARMESAN

6 servings/serving size: 3 oz.

An all-time favorite that creates an enticing aroma.

- **3 whole boneless, skinless chicken breasts, halved**
- **1/2 cup bread crumbs** (to further reduce sodium, see recipe, page 26, for homemade version)
- **1/3 cup Parmesan cheese**
- **1 tsp. dried oregano**
- **Fresh ground pepper**
- **2 egg substitute equivalents**
- **1/3 cup olive oil**
- **1 cup dry white wine**

1. Pound the chicken breasts until thin.
2. Combine the bread crumbs, Parmesan cheese, oregano, and pepper; set aside.
3. Beat eggs in a shallow dish. Dip chicken breasts into egg then crumb mixture, coating both sides.
4. Heat the oil in a skillet, add chicken, and saute until golden brown, about 3 to 4 minutes on each side. Remove chicken and set aside on a platter.
5. Drain fat from the skillet and add the wine, bringing the mixture to a boil while scraping down residue from the skillet. Pour sauce over the chicken and serve.

....

Lean Meat Exchange	4	Cholesterol	76 milligrams
Starch/Bread Exchange	1/2	Total Carbohydrate	7 grams
Fat Exchange	1/2	Dietary Fiber	0 grams
Calories	304	Sugars	1 gram
Total Fat	14 grams	Protein	31 grams
Saturated Fat	3 grams	Sodium	251 milligrams
Calories from Fat	124		

ALMOND CHICKEN

4 servings/serving size: 3 oz. chicken and 1/2 cup rice

A great dish for leftover chicken that is ready in less than 20 minutes.

- **2 Tbsp. olive oil**
- **1/2 cup sliced fresh mushrooms**
- **2 1/2 cups cubed precooked chicken**
- **1/4 cup flour**
- **Dash salt**
- **Fresh ground pepper**
- **1/4 cup white raisins**
- **1/3 cup sherry**
- **1 cup evaporated skimmed milk**
- **2 cups precooked rice, hot**
- **1/2 cup toasted slivered almonds**

1. In a large skillet, heat oil over medium heat. Add mushrooms and saute for 3 minutes.
2. Add chicken, flour, salt, and pepper. Add raisins and sherry and cook until sherry has been absorbed.
3. Add the milk and let simmer for 20 minutes. Arrange the rice on a serving platter, spoon chicken mixture over rice, top with slivered almonds, and serve.

....

Medium-Fat Meat Exchange 4	Cholesterol . . . . 80 milligrams
Starch/Bread Exchange 3	Total Carbohydrate . . . . 49 grams
Calories 531	Dietary Fiber . . . . 3 grams
Total Fat . . . . 20 grams	Sugars . . . . 14 grams
Saturated Fat . . . . 4 grams	Protein . . . . 37 grams
Calories from Fat 183	Sodium . . . . 191 milligrams

BAKED CHICKEN BREASTS SUPREME

6 servings/serving size: 3 oz. chicken

An especially nice dish that is slightly rich without the worry of excess fat. You'll need to start the night before.

- ♦ 3 whole boneless, skinless chicken breasts, halved
- ♦ 2 cups low-fat sour cream
- ♦ 1/4 cup lemon juice
- ♦ 4 tsp. Worcestershire sauce
- ♦ 1 tsp. celery salt
- ♦ 2 tsp. paprika
- ♦ 1 garlic clove, minced
- ♦ Dash salt
- ♦ Fresh ground pepper
- ♦ 1-3/4 cup fresh bread crumbs (see recipe, page 26)
- ♦ 1/4 cup olive oil
- ♦ Parsley sprigs
- ♦ 1 lemon, sliced

1. Wash chicken breasts under cold running water and pat dry.
2. Combine sour cream, lemon juice, Worcestershire, celery salt, paprika, garlic, and salt and pepper. Measure out 1/2 cup of marinade and reserve the rest.
3. Add chicken to the 1/2 cup of marinade and coat each piece well. Refrigerate overnight.
4. Remove chicken from the marinade, discard marinade, and roll chicken in bread crumbs, coating evenly. Arrange in a single layer in a large baking pan. Drizzle olive oil over the chicken breasts. Bake the chicken at 350 degrees, uncovered, for 45 minutes. Transfer to a serving platter, and serve with remaining marinade as a sauce and parsley and lemon slices as garnish.

....

Lean Meat Exchange 4	Cholesterol .... 72 milligrams
Starch/Bread Exchange 1	Total Carbohydrate .... 13 grams
Calories 312	Dietary Fiber .... 0 grams
Total Fat .... 15 grams	Sugars .... 6 grams
Saturated Fat .... 4 grams	Protein .... 30 grams
Calories from Fat 136	Sodium .... 282 milligrams

BAKED CHICKEN WITH HERBS

6 servings/serving size: 3–4 oz. chicken

Chicken with the nice flavor of pineapple and ginger.

- 1/2 tsp. dried rosemary
- Fresh ground pepper
- 3 lb. chicken parts, cut into serving pieces and skinned
- 1/2 cup pineapple juice
- 1/4 tsp. ground ginger
- 5 medium shallots, minced
- Paprika

1. Rub rosemary and pepper into the chicken pieces and arrange meaty side up in a 13x9x2-inch baking dish.
2. In a small bowl, combine the pineapple juice with ginger, mixing thoroughly; pour over chicken.
3. Add shallots and sprinkle paprika over chicken. Cover and bake at 350 degrees for 30 minutes. Baste with juices, uncover, and continue to cook for 25 to 30 minutes or until chicken is tender. Transfer to a serving platter and serve.

....

Lean Meat Exchange	3	Total Carbohydrate	4 grams
Calories	185	Dietary Fiber	0 grams
Total Fat	7 grams	Sugars	4 grams
Saturated Fat	2 grams	Protein	26 grams
Calories from Fat	59	Sodium	79 milligrams
Cholesterol	78 milligrams		

BAKED CHICKEN AND PEAS*

4 servings/serving size: 4 oz. chicken

Just add a salad, and you have dinner.

- 1 Tbsp. olive oil
- 2 Tbsp. lite soy sauce
- 1-1/2 tsp. paprika
- 1/2 tsp. basil
- 1/2 tsp. thyme
- 4 chicken thighs, skinned

- 1/4 lb. fresh mushrooms, sliced
- 1/2 cup low-sodium chicken broth
- 10 oz. frozen peas, thawed and drained

1. In a shallow 2-qt. casserole dish, combine oil, soy sauce, paprika, basil, and thyme. Add chicken thighs, and coat the chicken well.
2. Add mushrooms and chicken broth.
3. Cover and bake at 350 degrees for 50 minutes. Add peas; cover and continue baking for an additional 10 to 15 minutes or until peas are tender. Remove from oven and serve hot.

....

Lean Meat Exchange 3
Starch/Bread Exchange 1
Calories 252
Total Fat . . . . 11 grams
   Saturated Fat . . . . 2 grams
   Calories from Fat 98

Cholesterol . . . . 65 milligrams
Total Carbohydrate . . . . 15 grams
   Dietary Fiber . . . . 5 grams
   Sugars . . . . 6 grams
Protein . . . . 23 grams
Sodium . . . . 441 milligrams

* This recipe is relatively high in sodium.

CHICKEN PAPRIKA

8 servings/serving size: 3 oz.

*T*he classic Hungarian dish that is much lower in fat.

- 1 Tbsp. olive oil
- 1 large onion, minced
- 1 medium red pepper, julienned
- 1 cup sliced fresh mushrooms
- 1 cup water
- 1–2 tsp. paprika

- 2 Tbsp. lemon juice
- Dash salt
- Fresh ground pepper
- 4 whole boneless, skinless chicken breasts, halved
- 8 oz. low-fat sour cream

1. Heat oil in a large skillet. Add onion, pepper, and mushrooms and saute until tender, about 3 to 4 minutes.
2. Add water, paprika, lemon juice, salt, and pepper, blending well. Add chicken; cover and let simmer for 25 to 30 minutes or until chicken is tender. Stir in the sour cream and continue to cook for 1 to 2 minutes. Do not boil. Serve hot.

....

Lean Meat Exchange	3	Cholesterol	72 milligrams
Starch/Bread Exchange	1/2	Total Carbohydrate	9 grams
Vegetable Exchange	1	Dietary Fiber	1 gram
Calories	218	Sugars	6 grams
Total Fat	7 grams	Protein	29 grams
Saturated Fat	2 grams	Sodium	123 milligrams
Calories from Fat	62		

SPICY CHICKEN DRUMSTICKS

2 servings/serving size: 3 oz.

Serve these as a appetizer on a hot summer day.

- ◆ **1/4 cup plain low-fat yogurt**
- ◆ **2 Tbsp. hot pepper sauce**
- ◆ **4 chicken drumsticks, skinned**

- ◆ **1/4 cup bread crumbs** (to further reduce sodium, see recipe, page 26, for homemade version)

1. In a shallow dish, combine yogurt and hot pepper sauce, mixing well. Add drumsticks, turning to coat and cover and marinate in the refrigerator for 2 to 4 hours.
2. Remove drumsticks from marinade, dredge in bread crumbs, and place in a baking dish. Bake at 350 degrees for 40 to 50 minutes. Transfer to a serving platter and serve.

....

Lean Meat Exchange 3	Cholesterol . . . . 76 milligrams
Starch/Bread Exchange 1/2	Total Carbohydrate . . . . 10 grams
Calories 204	Dietary Fiber . . . . 1 gram
Total Fat . . . . 6 grams	Sugars . . . . 1 gram
Saturated Fat . . . . 2 grams	Protein . . . . 26 grams
Calories from Fat 51	Sodium . . . . 221 milligrams

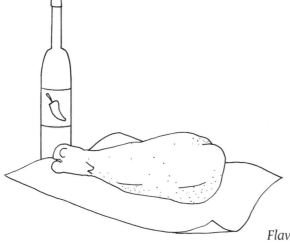

OVEN-BAKED CHICKEN TENDERS

4 servings/serving size: 3 oz.

Kids will love these bite-sized morsels of crunchy chicken that are baked, not fried. Serve with Marinara Sauce (see recipe, page 8).

- ◆ 2 whole boneless, skinless chicken breasts, halved
- ◆ 2 egg whites, beaten
- ◆ 1/2 cup whole-wheat cracker crumbs
- ◆ 1 tsp. dried basil
- ◆ 1/2 tsp. dried oregano
- ◆ 1/2 tsp. dried thyme
- ◆ 2 tsp. fresh grated Parmesan cheese
- ◆ 1 tsp. paprika

1. Cut each chicken breast into 2x1/2-inch strips.
2. Dip each strip into egg whites.
3. On a flat plate or in a plastic bag, combine cracker crumbs with spices and cheese. Add chicken strips, and coat with the crumb mixture.
4. On a nonstick cookie sheet, place chicken strips side by side in one layer. Bake at 350 degrees for 10 to 12 minutes until golden and crunchy.

....

Lean Meat Exchange	3	
Starch/Bread Exchange	1/2	
Calories	197	
Total Fat	5 grams	
Saturated Fat	1 gram	
Calories from Fat	46	

Cholesterol	73 milligrams	
Total Carbohydrate	6 grams	
Dietary Fiber	0 grams	
Sugars	0 grams	
Protein	29 grams	
Sodium	181 milligrams	

CHICKEN OR TURKEY BURGERS

6 servings/serving size: 3–4 oz.

When you tire of the same old hamburgers, try these for a delightful change.

- ◆ **1-1/4 lb. ground chicken or turkey**
- ◆ **1 egg substitute equivalent**
- ◆ **1/4 tsp. onion powder**
- ◆ **1/4 tsp. dried thyme**
- ◆ **1/2 tsp. poultry seasoning**
- ◆ **1/4 tsp. dried sage**

- ◆ **Dash salt**
- ◆ **Fresh ground pepper**
- ◆ **6 Tbsp. plain dried bread crumbs** (to further reduce sodium, see recipe, page 26, for homemade version)

1. In a medium bowl, combine all the ingredients except bread crumbs. Scoop meat into 6 patties and press each one lightly into the bread crumbs.
2. Prepare an outside grill or oven broiler and grill or broil 6 inches from heat for 4 to 5 minutes per side until cooked through. Serve warm on split buns and your favorite condiments.

....

Lean Meat Exchange 3
Starch/Bread Exchange 1/2
Calories 188
Total Fat . . . . 10 grams
   Saturated Fat . . . . 3 grams
   Calories from Fat 88

Cholesterol . . . . 48 milligrams
Total Carbohydrate . . . . 5 grams
   Dietary Fiber . . . . 0 grams
   Sugars . . . . 0 grams
Protein . . . . 19 grams
Sodium . . . . 152 milligrams

SUMMER CHICKEN KABOBS

4 servings/serving size: 3 oz. chicken

Although the name denotes warm weather, try these kabobs when squash is fresh.

- 1/4 cup lime juice
- 2 Tbsp. olive oil
- 1 Tbsp. minced parsley
- 1/2 tsp. dried thyme
- 1 garlic clove, minced
- Fresh ground pepper
- 2 whole boneless, skinless chicken breasts, cubed

- 1 small yellow squash, cut into 2-inch pieces
- 1 small zucchini, cut into 1-inch pieces
- 4 large cherry tomatoes

1. In a shallow dish, combine lime juice, oil, parsley, thyme, garlic, and pepper; mix well.
2. Add chicken, yellow squash, and zucchini, tossing to coat. Cover and refrigerate for 2 hours.
3. Alternate chicken, squash, and zucchini onto each of the skewers. Grill 4 inches from heat for 10 minutes, turning frequently. Add cherry tomatoes to each skewer during the last 1 minute of cooking. Remove from heat and serve.

....

Lean Meat Exchange 3	Cholesterol . . . . 72 milligrams
Vegetable Exchange 1	Total Carbohydrate . . . . 4 grams
Calories 189	Dietary Fiber . . . . 1 gram
Total Fat . . . . 7 grams	Sugars . . . . 2 grams
Saturated Fat . . . . 1 gram	Protein . . . . 27 grams
Calories from Fat 59	Sodium . . . . 67 milligrams

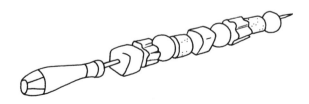

INDOOR BARBECUED TURKEY

10 servings/serving size: 3 oz. meat

Have turkey anytime. This is slowly roasted turkey breast in a beer-mustard sauce.

- **5-lb. (including bone) turkey breast**
- **1 Tbsp. prepared mustard**
- **1/2 cup light beer**
- **1/4 cup red wine vinegar**
- **3/4 cup ketchup**
- **1 Tbsp. no-added-salt tomato paste**
- **1/2 cup spicy no-added-salt tomato juice** (or spice up mild juice with several drops of hot pepper sauce)
- **Fresh ground pepper**

1. Spread turkey breast with mustard. Combine beer, vinegar, ketchup, tomato paste, and tomato juice in a small bowl.
2. Pour mixture over turkey, then sprinkle with pepper. Roast, covered, for 1-1/2 hours at 350 degrees. Remove cover and roast an additional 1 hour, basting occasionally. Transfer to a serving platter and serve.

....

Lean Meat Exchange 3		Total Carbohydrate . . . . 2 grams	
Calories 155		Dietary Fiber . . . . 0 grams	
Total Fat . . . . 1 gram		Sugars . . . . 1 gram	
Saturated Fat . . . . 0 grams		Protein . . . . 33 grams	
Calories from Fat 8		Sodium . . . . 148 milligrams	
Cholesterol . . . . 92 milligrams			

HOMEMADE SEASONED BREAD CRUMBS

8 servings/serving size: 1/4 cup

These homemade bread crumbs are much lower in sodium than the store-bought variety, and very easy to make.

- 1/3 loaf low-calorie store-bought bread
- 2 tsp. garlic powder
- 1 tsp. dried basil
- 1 tsp. dried oregano
- 1 tsp. onion powder
- 1/4 tsp. paprika
- 1/4 tsp. salt
- 1/4 tsp. pepper

1. Leave bread on the kitchen counter to dry for 2 days. Remove the crusts, and tear the bread into bite-size pieces.
2. Place bread in a food processor or blender with spices and blend to make crumbs.

. . . .

Starch/Bread Exchange 1/2	Total Carbohydrate . . . . 9 grams
Calories 42	Dietary Fiber . . . . 2 grams
Total Fat . . . . 1 gram	Sugars . . . . 1 gram
Saturated Fat . . . . 0 grams	Protein . . . . 2 grams
Calories from Fat 5	Sodium . . . . 158 milligrams
Cholesterol . . . . 0 milligrams	

SIMPLE SEAFOODS

HINTS FOR BUYING AND PREPARING DELICIOUS FISH

♦ When buying whole fish, look for bright, clear eyes; red gills; bright, tight scales; and shiny skins. Stale fish have cloudy, sunken eyes; with age, gill color fades to a light pink. The flesh should be firm and springy. When buying fillets, look for freshly cut flesh, firm in texture, without a dried or brown look. When buying frozen fillets, the wrapping should be made of moisture-proof material and have little or no odor. Look for solidly frozen flesh with clear color, free of ice crystals. Discoloration, a brownish tinge, or a covering of ice crystals all indicate that the fish may have been thawed and refrozen.

♦ To store fresh fish, keep fish and shellfish loosely wrapped in the refrigerator and cook within one day. To store frozen fish, keep fish in the original wrapper and use immediately after thawing. Never thaw and refreeze fish, because this will cause moisture loss and texture and flavor changes.

♦ The best way to thaw frozen fish is to leave it in its original wrappings and thaw it in the refrigerator or in cold water. Thawing at room temperature can cause sogginess. Drain the fish well after unwrapping it and blot it dry with paper towels.

HALIBUT SUPREME

6 servings/serving size: 3 oz.

Halibut with a crunchy almond topping.

- Nonstick cooking spray
- 1-1/2 lb. halibut steaks
- 1 cup sliced mushrooms
- 1 Tbsp. olive oil
- 1 small onion, finely chopped
- 3 Tbsp. white wine
- 3/4 cup water
- Dash salt
- Fresh ground pepper
- 1/4 cup toasted almond slivers
- 1 Tbsp. chopped parsley

1. Coat a 13x9x2-inch baking dish with cooking spray, and place halibut steaks in baking dish.
2. Add the remaining ingredients, except almonds and parsley, and bake at 325 degrees, basting frequently, for 25 minutes until fish flakes easily with a fork.
3. Remove from oven and top the halibut steaks with toasted almond slivers. Garnish with parsley.

. . . .

Lean Meat Exchange	3	Cholesterol	37 milligrams
Vegetable Exchange	1	Total Carbohydrate	3 grams
Calories	186	Dietary Fiber	1 gram
Total Fat	7 grams	Sugars	2 grams
Saturated Fat	1 gram	Protein	25 grams
Calories from Fat	66	Sodium	85 milligrams

FLOUNDER PARMESAN

4 servings/serving size: 3 oz.

*I*nstead of frying, why not have crusty baked fish?

- 1 lb. flounder fillets
- 1/4 cup fresh grated Parmesan cheese
- 1 tsp. dried oregano
- 1/4 tsp. dried basil
- 1 Tbsp. minced onion

- 1 tsp. garlic powder
- 2 tsp. paprika
- 2 Tbsp. finely minced parsley
- Fresh ground pepper
- 8 oz. low-fat sour cream

1. Place fish fillets in a baking dish.
2. Combine the remaining ingredients and spread over fish. Bake for 12 to 15 minutes at 375 degrees. Transfer to a platter and serve.

Lean Meat Exchange 3
Starch/Bread Exchange 1/2
Calories 203
Total Fat . . . . 7 grams
   Saturated Fat . . . . 3 grams
   Calories from Fat 60
Cholesterol . . . . 61 milligrams
Total Carbohydrate . . . . 8 grams
   Dietary Fiber . . . . 0 grams
   Sugars . . . . 8 grams
Protein . . . . 27 grams
Sodium . . . . 261 grams

ITALIAN FILLETS OF SOLE

6 servings/serving size: 3–4 oz.

*I*talian herbs and Parmesan cheese makes this dish special.

- 1-1/2 lb. sole fillets
- Fresh ground pepper
- 1/2 cup grated Parmesan cheese
- 1 tsp. dried oregano
- 1 tsp. dried basil
- 1 tsp. paprika
- 2 tsp. garlic powder
- 1 tsp. onion powder
- Nonstick cooking spray
- 2 Tbsp. olive oil
- 1 large lemon, cut into wedges

1. Wash fish fillets and pat dry with paper towels. In a sealable plastic bag, combine remaining ingredients except olive oil and lemon.
2. Add fillets one at a time to the bag, and shake until the fish is coated. Set coated fish on a plate, and place plate in the refrigerator, covered, for 1 hour to allow coating to adhere to the fish.
3. Coat a large skillet with cooking spray, then add the olive oil. When oil is hot, add fish and quickly saute for 3 minutes per side, turning fillets very carefully. Transfer to a serving platter and serve garnished with lemon wedges.

••

Lean Meat Exchange 3
Calories 173
Total Fat . . . . 8 grams
   Saturated Fat . . . . 2 grams
   Calories from Fat 70
Cholesterol . . . . 66 milligrams

Total Carbohydrate . . . . 0 grams
   Dietary Fiber . . . . 0 grams
   Sugars . . . . 0 grams
Protein . . . . 24 grams
Sodium . . . . 217 milligrams

BAKED FISH IN FOIL

8 servings/serving size: 3 oz.

*P*reparing fish in foil is the easiest and most flavorful method of cooking.

- ◆ 3 lb. whole red snapper or bass, cleaned
- ◆ 1 medium garlic clove, minced
- ◆ 1/4 cup olive oil
- ◆ Fresh ground pepper
- ◆ 1/2 tsp. dried thyme
- ◆ 1 tsp. flour

- ◆ 1/2 lb. large shrimp, peeled and deveined
- ◆ 1/2 lb. sliced mushrooms
- ◆ 3 Tbsp. lemon juice
- ◆ 1/2 cup dry white wine
- ◆ 1/4 cup minced parsley
- ◆ 1 tsp. grated lemon peel

1. Wash fish, inside and out, under cold running water, and pat dry with paper towels.
2. In a small bowl, combine garlic, olive oil, pepper, thyme, and flour and mix well.
3. Place fish on a double thickness of heavy aluminum foil. In the cavity of the fish, place 1 Tbsp. garlic mixture, 4 shrimp, and 1/2 cup sliced mushrooms. Sprinkle with 1 Tbsp. lemon juice and 2 Tbsp. wine.
4. Dot top of fish with remaining garlic mixture and arrange remaining shrimp and mushrooms on top. Sprinkle with remaining lemon juice and wine, parsley, and lemon peel.
5. Bring the long sides of the foil together over the fish and secure with a double fold. Fold both ends of foil upward several times.
6. Place fish on a cookie sheet; bake at 375 degrees for 30 to 35 minutes. Transfer to a serving platter and serve.

....

Lean Meat Exchange	3	Cholesterol	72 milligrams
Fat Exchange	1/2	Total Carbohydrate	2 grams
Calories	194	Dietary Fiber	1 gram
Total Fat	9 grams	Sugars	0 grams
Saturated Fat	1 gram	Protein	27 grams
Calories from Fat	77	Sodium	88 milligrams

HERB-BROILED COD

4 servings/serving size: 3 oz.

*T*arragon gives some zip to mild-mannered cod.

- 2 Tbsp. olive oil
- 1 Tbsp. tarragon vinegar
- 1 tsp. lemon juice
- 2 Tbsp. fresh parsley

- 1 tsp. fresh minced tarragon
- Fresh ground pepper
- 4 cod fillets (about 4 oz. each)

1. Combine all the ingredients except fish.
2. Place fish on the grill or under the broiler. Brush some of the tarragon mixture over the fillets and cook for 5 minutes. Turn the fillets over and brush with the remaining tarragon mixture. Cook for another 5 minutes. Serve.

- -

Lean Meat Exchange 3	Total Carbohydrate . . . . 0 grams
Calories 151	Dietary Fiber . . . . 0 grams
Total Fat . . . . 7 grams	Sugars . . . . 0 grams
Saturated Fat . . . . 7 grams	Protein . . . . 20 grams
Calories from Fat 66	Sodium . . . . 67 milligrams
Cholesterol . . . . 48 milligrams	

FISH FILLETS WITH TOMATOES

4 servings/serving size: 3 oz.

*U*se any white fish you want. This is good with orange roughy, *flounder, sole, or perch.*

- ◆ 1 medium tomato, minced
- ◆ 1 Tbsp. minced onion
- ◆ 1/2 tsp. fresh dill
- ◆ 1/4 tsp. dried basil
- ◆ 1 lb. fish fillets

- ◆ 2 Tbsp. olive oil
- ◆ 1 Tbsp. lemon juice
- ◆ 1/4 cup water
- ◆ 1 lemon, cut into wedges

1. Combine tomato, onion, dill, and basil.
2. Place fillets in a skillet and brush with the olive oil. Spoon tomato mixture over fish. Add lemon juice and water.
3. Simmer fillets over medium heat for 8 to 10 minutes. Transfer to a serving platter and garnish with lemon wedges.

••

Lean Meat Exchange 3
Calories 167
Total Fat . . . . 8 grams
    Saturated Fat . . . . 1 gram
    Calories from Fat 73
Cholesterol . . . . 58 milligrams

Total Carbohydrate . . . . 2 grams
    Dietary Fiber . . . . 0 grams
    Sugars . . . . 1 gram
Protein . . . . 21 grams
Sodium . . . . 94 milligrams

BAKED SHRIMP*

4 servings/serving size: 3 oz. (about 4 large shrimp)

*A*lthough great for every day, don't hesitate to prepare this for guests, too.

- ◆ **16 large shrimp**
- ◆ **2 Tbsp. olive oil**
- ◆ **1–2 Tbsp. water**
- ◆ **1/2 cup chopped parsley**
- ◆ **3 garlic cloves, minced**

- ◆ **1 cup bread crumbs** (to further reduce sodium, see recipe, page 26, for homemade version)
- ◆ **2 tsp. paprika**
- ◆ **1 large lemon, cut into wedges**

1. With a small knife, cut down the back of the shrimp, but not all the way through, and flatten slightly. Place shrimp in a baking dish.
2. Combine olive oil, water, parsley, garlic, bread crumbs, and paprika. Mix thoroughly, and spoon mixture on each shrimp. Bake for 10 minutes at 400 degrees and garnish with lemon wedges.

. . . .

Lean Meat Exchange 3	Cholesterol . . . . 167 milligrams
Starch/Bread Exchange 1	Total Carbohydrate . . . . 21 grams
Calories 255	Dietary Fiber . . . . 1 gram
Total Fat . . . . 9 grams	Sugars . . . . 2 grams
Saturated Fat . . . . 2 grams	Protein . . . . 22 grams
Calories from Fat 83	Sodium . . . . 426 milligrams

* This recipe is relatively high in sodium.

BOILED SHRIMP

6 servings/serving size: 4 oz.

A good basic recipe to prepare shrimp for cocktail sauce.

- 4 bay leaves
- 20 peppercorns
- 12 whole cloves
- 1 tsp. cayenne pepper
- 1 tsp. dried marjoram
- 1/2 tsp. dried basil
- 1/4 tsp. dried thyme
- 1/8 tsp. caraway seeds
- 1 tsp. mustard seeds
- 1/8 tsp. cumin seeds
- 1/4 tsp. fennel seeds
- 8 cups water
- 1 large lemon, quartered
- 1 garlic clove, minced
- 2 lb. large shrimp, peeled and deveined

1. In a double or triple thickness of cheesecloth, combine all the spices (first 11 ingredients). Secure the packet with a piece of string.
2. Combine water, lemon, garlic, and spice bag together in a dutch oven. Bring the water to a boil, reduce the heat, and simmer for 3 minutes.
3. Add shrimp and return to a boil. Boil shrimp for 3 to 5 minutes. Drain thoroughly and chill. Serve with cocktail sauce.

....

Lean Meat Exchange 2
Calories 113
Total Fat . . . . 1 gram
   Saturated Fat . . . . 0 grams
   Calories from Fat 11
Cholesterol . . . . 222 milligrams

Total Carbohydrate . . . . 0 grams
   Dietary Fiber . . . . 0 grams
   Sugars . . . . 0 grams
Protein . . . . 24 grams
Sodium . . . . 255 milligrams

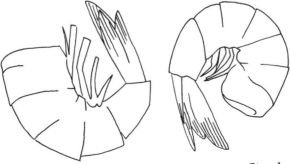

BROILED SALMON STEAKS

4 servings/serving size: 3 oz.

When you're in the mood for a light dinner with no fuss, turn to this basic recipe for salmon. Serve with a little nonfat sour cream or plain yogurt flavored with dill, parsley, and minced garlic.

- 1/4 cup olive oil
- 1/2 tsp. fresh dill
- 1/4 tsp. fresh thyme
- 1 Tbsp. lemon juice
- 1 Tbsp. fresh chopped parsley
- 1/4 cup minced scallions
- 1 lb. fresh salmon steaks

1. In a bowl, combine oil, dill, thyme, lemon juice, parsley, and scallions. Add fish and let marinate for 30 minutes.
2. Remove fish from marinade, and broil each steak for 4 to 5 minutes per side until fish is no longer translucent. Place on a platter and serve.

Lean Meat Exchange	3	Total Carbohydrate	0 grams
Calories	199	Dietary Fiber	0 grams
Total Fat	11 grams	Sugars	0 grams
Saturated Fat	2 grams	Protein	23 grams
Calories from Fat	97	Sodium	51 milligrams
Cholesterol	42 milligrams		

GRILLED SHARK

4 servings/serving size: 3 oz.

*B*ecause shark has flavor by itself, this recipe is just brings out the natural flavor without a lot of complicated ingredients.

- 1 lb. shark fillets
- 3 Tbsp. fresh lime juice
- Fresh ground pepper
- 2 tsp. olive oil

- 1 Tbsp. fresh chopped mint
- 1 Tbsp. fresh chopped cilantro
- 1 garlic clove, minced

1. Wash the shark fillets and combine with the lime juice. Sprinkle with pepper. Marinate refrigerated for 1 to 2 hours.
2. Combine oil, mint, cilantro, and garlic. Brush fillets with mixture. Grill over medium heat for 6 to 8 minutes, turning once. Transfer to a platter and serve.

....

Lean Meat Exchange 3	Total Carbohydrates . . . . 1 gram
Calories 161	Dietary Fiber . . . . 0 grams
Total Fat . . . . 7 grams	Sugars . . . . 1 gram
Saturated Fat . . . . 2 grams	Protein . . . . 23 grams
Calories from Fat 62	Sodium . . . . 103 milligrams
Cholesterol . . . . 44 milligrams	

GRILLED SWORDFISH WITH ROSEMARY

4 servings/serving size: 3 oz.

When preparing swordfish, no need to fuss. Just a few touches here and there produces wonderful fish.

- ◆ **2 scallions, thinly sliced**
- ◆ **2 Tbsp. olive oil**
- ◆ **2 Tbsp. white wine vinegar**

- ◆ **1 tsp. fresh rosemary**
- ◆ **4 swordfish steaks (3–4 oz. each)**

1. Combine the marinade ingredients, and pour over the swordfish steaks. Let marinate for 30 minutes.
2. Remove steaks from marinade, and grill for 5 to 7 minutes per side, brushing with marinade. Transfer to a serving platter and serve.

....

Lean Meat Exchange 3	Total Carbohydrate . . . . 0 grams
Fat Exchange 1/2	Dietary Fiber . . . . 0 grams
Total Fat . . . . 11 grams	Sugars . . . . 0 grams
Saturated Fat . . . . 2 grams	Protein . . . . 22 grams
Calories from Fat 101	Sodium . . . . 99 milligrams
Cholesterol . . . . 42 milligrams	

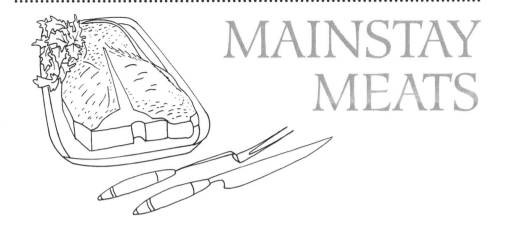

APPLE CINNAMON PORK CHOPS

2 servings/serving size: 3 oz. meat plus apples

This dish will remind you of a crisp fall evening.

- ◆ 1 Tbsp. canola oil
- ◆ 1 large apple, sliced
- ◆ 1 tsp. cinnamon
- ◆ 1/4 tsp. nutmeg
- ◆ 2 pork chops (4 oz. each), trimmed of fat

1. In a medium nonstick skillet, heat the canola oil. Add apple slices and saute until just tender. Sprinkle with cinnamon and nutmeg, remove from heat and keep warm.
2. Place pork chops in skillet, and cook thoroughly. Remove pork chops from skillet, arrange on a serving platter, spoon apple slices on top, and serve.

Medium-Fat Meat Exchange	3	Cholesterol	69 milligrams
Fat Exchange	1/2	Total Carbohydrate	19 grams
Fruit Exchange	1	Dietary Fiber	3 grams
Calories	318	Sugars	16 grams
Total Fat	16 grams	Protein	25 grams
Saturated Fat	4 grams	Sodium	49 milligrams
Calories from Fat	140		

BASIL PORK CHOPS

4 servings/serving size: 3 oz. meat

*S*erve these Italian-accented chops with fresh pasta.

- ◆ **4 pork chops, trimmed of fat (about 5 oz. each)**
- ◆ **1 cup no-added-salt tomato sauce**
- ◆ **2 Tbsp. white wine**
- ◆ **1 Tbsp. tomato paste**

- ◆ **1 Tbsp. fresh minced basil**
- ◆ **1 tsp. fresh minced oregano**
- ◆ **1 clove garlic, minced**
- ◆ **1 Tbsp. minced parsley**
- ◆ **Fresh ground pepper**

1. In a large skillet, brown the pork chops, and drain any fat.
2. Add the remaining ingredients, cover, and simmer for 45 minutes or until pork chops are tender. Remove from heat and transfer to a serving platter.

....

Lean Meat Exchange	3	Cholesterol	69 milligrams
Vegetable Exchange	1	Total Carbohydrate	6 grams
Calories	205	Dietary Fiber	1 gram
Total Fat	8 grams	Sugars	2 grams
Saturated Fat	3 grams	Protein	26 grams
Calories from Fat	74	Sodium	94 milligrams

STIR-FRIED PORK TENDERLOINS

6 servings/servings size: 3 oz.

The secret to this dish is not to overcook it.

- 1 lb. pork tenderloins, cut in thin strips
- 1 Tbsp. vegetable oil
- 1 Tbsp. oyster sauce (found in the Chinese foods section of the grocery store)
- 1 Tbsp. cornstarch
- 1/2 cup low-sodium chicken broth
- 1 Tbsp. lite soy sauce
- 1 cup fresh snow peas, trimmed
- 1/2 cup sliced water chestnuts, drained
- 1/2 cup minced red pepper
- 1/4 cup sliced scallions

1. In a large skillet or wok, heat oil. Stir-fry pork until strips are no longer pink.
2. Combine oyster sauce, cornstarch, chicken broth, and soy sauce in a measuring cup. Add to the pork, and cook until sauce thickens.
3. Add vegetables, cover, and steam for 2 to 3 minutes. Serve.

....

Lean Meat Exchange 2	Cholesterol . . . . 48 milligrams
Vegetable Exchange 1	Total Carbohydrate . . . . 7 grams
Calories 155	Dietary Fiber . . . . 1 gram
Total Fat . . . . 6 grams	Sugars . . . . 3 grams
Saturated Fat . . . . 1 gram	Protein . . . . 18 grams
Calories from Fat 53	Sodium . . . . 151 milligrams

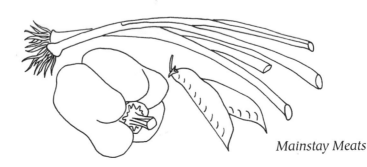

PORK CHOPS MILANESE*

4 servings/serving size: 1 pork chop (about 2 oz. meat)

You will win rave reviews when you prepare these.

- ◆ **1 cup fresh bread crumbs** (see recipe, page 26)
- ◆ **1/2 cup grated Parmesan cheese**
- ◆ **1/2 cup flour**
- ◆ **2 egg substitute equivalents, slightly beaten**
- ◆ **4 pork chops (3–4 oz. each)**
- ◆ **3 Tbsp. low-calorie margarine**
- ◆ **1 large lemon, cut into wedges**

1. Combine bread crumbs and Parmesan cheese in a shallow bowl. Dip the pork chops in flour, then eggs, and dredge in bread crumb mixture.
2. Melt margarine in a large skillet. Add pork chops and brown on both sides. Reduce heat, cover, and simmer for 3 to 5 minutes. Remove cover, and cook 5 to 10 minutes more until pork is completely cooked.
3. Squeeze 2 or 3 lemon wedges over chops. Transfer to a serving platter, garnish with remaining lemon wedges, and serve.

· ·

Lean Meat Exchange 3
Starch/Bread Exchange 1-1/2
Fat Exchange 1
Calories 332
Total Fat . . . . 14 grams
  Saturated Fat . . . . 5 grams
  Calories from Fat 122

Cholesterol . . . . 54 milligrams
Total Carbohydrate . . . . 24 grams
  Dietary Fiber . . . . 1 gram
  Sugars . . . . 2 grams
Protein . . . . 26 grams
Sodium . . . . 515 milligrams

* This recipe is relatively high in sodium.

BEEF STROGANOFF

8 servings/serving size: 3 oz. meat plus 1/2 cup noodles

*H*earty homestyle food that never goes out of style.

- ◆ **4 Tbsp. olive oil**
- ◆ **2 Tbsp. minced onion**
- ◆ **2 lb. lean sirloin steak, pounded and cut into 1-inch cubes**
- ◆ **1/2 lb. fresh mushrooms, sliced**
- ◆ **Fresh ground pepper**
- ◆ **Dash nutmeg**
- ◆ **1 cup low-fat sour cream**
- ◆ **9 oz. uncooked noodles**

1. In a large skillet over medium heat, heat oil and add onion and beef and saute for 5 minutes. Add mushrooms, pepper, and nutmeg.
2. Reduce the heat to low, and add sour cream, stirring constantly until well blended.
3. Cook noodles in boiling water for 9 to 10 minutes. Drain. Place noodles on a serving dish and place beef mixture on top. Serve.

Lean Meat Exchange 3
Starch/Bread Exchange 2
Fat Exchange 1
Calories 369
Total Fat . . . . 14 grams
   Saturated Fat . . . . 4 grams
   Calories from Fat 127

Cholesterol . . . . 89 milligrams
Total Carbohydrate . . . . 28 grams
   Dietary Fiber . . . . 1 gram
   Sugars . . . . 6 grams
Protein . . . . 32 grams
Sodium . . . . 100 milligrams

HERBED POT ROAST

8 servings/serving size: 3 oz.

This lean roast simmers slowly in an herb marinade.

- 1 Tbsp. olive oil
- 2 lb. lean boneless beef roast
- Fresh ground pepper
- 1/2 cup water
- 1/3 cup dry sherry
- 1/4 cup ketchup
- 1 garlic clove, minced
- 1/4 tsp. dry mustard
- 1/4 tsp. marjoram
- 1/4 tsp. dried rosemary
- 1/4 tsp. dried thyme
- 2 medium onions, sliced
- 1 bay leaf
- 16 oz. canned sliced mushrooms, undrained

1. Add olive oil to a large Dutch oven over medium heat. Sprinkle roast with pepper, and brown roast on all sides.
2. Combine water, sherry, ketchup, garlic, mustard, marjoram, rosemary, and thyme in a small bowl, and pour over roast. Add onions and bay leaf, cover, and simmer for 2 to 3 hours, until roast is tender.
3. Add mushrooms and continue simmering until heated. Remove bay leaf. Transfer roast to a platter, slice, and serve.

....

Lean Meat Exchange	3	Cholesterol	87 milligrams
Starch/Bread Exchange	1/2	Total Carbohydrate	7 grams
Fat Exchange	1/2	Dietary Fiber	1 gram
Calories	232	Sugars	3 grams
Total Fat	9 grams	Protein	29 grams
Saturated Fat	3 grams	Sodium	288 milligrams
Calories from Fat	82		

MEAT LOAF

8 servings/serving size: 3 oz.

By making meat loaf with beef, veal, and pork, you get a flavor that is out of this world.

- **1 lb. lean ground beef**
- **1/2 lb. ground veal**
- **1/2 lb. ground pork**
- **3/4 cup bread crumbs** (to further reduce sodium, see recipe, page 26, for homemade version)
- **1 cup skim milk**

- **1 egg substitute equivalents**
- **1 medium onion, chopped** (for variety, add 1/4 cup shredded carrot, 2 Tbsp. chopped green pepper, and/or 1/4 cup sliced celery)
- **16 oz. canned stewed tomatoes**

1. In a large bowl, combine all ingredients except tomatoes. Place into loaf pan, and pour tomatoes over the top.
2. Bake at 350 degrees for 1 hour. Remove from oven, drain fat, slice, and serve.

- -

Lean Meat Exchange 4	Cholesterol . . . . 82 milligrams
Starch/Bread Exchange 1	Total Carbohydrate . . . . 15 grams
Calories 284	Dietary Fiber . . . . 1 gram
Total Fat . . . . 12 grams	Sugars . . . . 6 grams
Saturated Fat . . . . 5 grams	Protein . . . . 27 grams
Calories from Fat 111	Sodium . . . . 328 milligrams

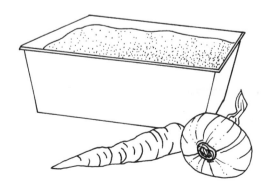

HEARTY CHILI

8 servings/serving size: 1 cup

*E*veryone loves chili, and the addition of vegetables makes it more of a meal.

- 1 Tbsp. olive oil
- 1 cup chopped onion
- 3 garlic cloves, minced
- 1 lb. lean ground beef
- 28 oz. coarsely chopped tomatoes (reserve juice)
- 2 cups cooked kidney, pinto, or black beans, drained and rinsed
- 3 Tbsp. chili powder

- 1 Tbsp. ground cumin
- 1 Tbsp. ground oregano
- 1/4 tsp. cloves
- 1/4 tsp. allspice
- 1/4 tsp. cinnamon
- 2 jalapeño peppers, minced
- 1 cup diced green peppers
- 1 cup sliced carrots
- 1 cup cooked corn kernels

1. In large pot, heat oil over medium heat. Add onion and garlic, and saute for 5 minutes. Add ground beef, and saute until beef is no longer pink. Drain the fat.
2. Add tomatoes, beans, and seasonings, and simmer for 45 minutes.
3. Add jalapeños, peppers, carrots, and corn, and simmer for 30 minutes more. Serve.

....

Medium-Fat Meat Exchange	1	Cholesterol	35 milligrams
Starch/Bread Exchange	1	Total Carbohydrate	26 grams
Vegetable Exchange	2	Dietary Fiber	6 grams
Fat Exchange	1	Sugars	9 grams
Calories	253	Protein	17 grams
Total Fat	10 grams	Sodium	310 milligrams
Saturated Fat	3 grams		
Calories from Fat	92		

STUFFED CABBAGE LEAVES

6 servings/serving size: 1 stuffed cabbage plus 1/6 of cabbage wedges

A *homey meal that is perfect during long cold winters.*

- **1 medium head green cabbage**
- **1/2 cup instant white rice**
- **1 lb. lean ground sirloin**
- **Dash nutmeg**
- **1/4 tsp. salt**
- **Fresh ground pepper**
- **1 small onion, chopped**
- **2 cups water**

1. In a large saucepan, place whole cabbage head and cover with water. Bring to a boil, lower the heat, and simmer for 3 to 4 minutes. Remove cabbage from the water, and carefully remove 6 whole outer leaves from head. Cut remainder of cabbage into wedges.
2. In a large mixing bowl, combine remaining ingredients, except water, and shape mixture into 6 balls.
3. Wrap a cabbage leaf around each ball, and secure with toothpicks. Place cabbage rolls and wedges in a saucepan, add water, cover, and bring to a boil. Lower heat, and simmer for 25 to 30 minutes. Transfer to a serving platter, discard toothpicks, and serve.

....

Lean Meat Exchange 2	Cholesterol . . . . 46 milligrams
Starch/Bread Exchange 1/2	Total Carbohydrate . . . . 15 grams
Vegetable Exchange 1	Dietary Fiber . . . . 5 grams
Calories 169	Sugars . . . . 3 grams
Total Fat . . . . 4 grams	Protein . . . . 19 grams
Saturated Fat . . . . 1 gram	Sodium . . . . 146 milligrams
Calories from Fat 37	

ROAST BEEF WITH CARAWAY SEEDS

8 servings/serving size: 3 oz.

Serve this hearty dish with cabbage and noodles.

- ♦ **3/4 cup chopped onion**
- ♦ **1 Tbsp. caraway seeds**
- ♦ **2 lb. lean boneless chuck roast**
- ♦ **1 Tbsp. olive oil**
- ♦ **1/3 cup red wine vinegar**
- ♦ **1 cup unsweetened apple juice**
- ♦ **1 Tbsp. minced parsley**
- ♦ **1/2 cup water**

1. In a small bowl, combine 1/4 cup onion and caraway seeds and press into roast.
2. In a medium saucepan, saute remaining onion in olive oil. Place roast in a roasting pan and add the sauteed onion.
3. Add vinegar, apple juice, parsley, and water. Bake roast at 325 degrees uncovered for 1 to 1-1/2 hours, basting frequently. Transfer roast to a platter and slice.

Lean Meat Exchange	3	Cholesterol	87 milligrams
Starch/Bread Exchange	1/2	Total Carbohydrate	6 grams
Calories	224	Dietary Fiber	0 grams
Total Fat	9 grams	Sugars	5 grams
Saturated Fat	3 grams	Protein	28 grams
Calories from Fat	81	Sodium	59 milligrams

BEEF SHISH KABOBS

8 servings/serving size: 3 oz. beef plus vegetables

*W*hile the kabobs are cooking, simmer some rice, and add a salad for a complete meal.

- 1/3 cup olive oil
- 1/4 cup red wine vinegar
- 1 Tbsp. lite soy sauce
- 1 garlic clove, minced
- 1 Tbsp. lemon juice
- Fresh ground pepper
- 2 lb. lean beef, cubed

- 2 large bell peppers, red and green, cut into 1-inch pieces
- 1 lb. mushrooms, stemmed
- 1 large tomato, cut into wedges
- 1 medium onion, quartered

1. Combine marinade ingredients (first 6 ingredients), and pour over the beef cubes. Let marinate 3 to 4 hours or overnight.
2. Place beef on skewers, alternating with peppers, mushroom caps, tomatoes, and onions. Grill over medium heat, turning and basting with marinade. Arrange skewers on a platter to serve.

....

Lean Meat Exchange 3	Cholesterol .... 69 milligrams
Fat Exchange 1	Total Carbohydrate .... 9 grams
Vegetable Exchange 2	Dietary Fiber .... 2 gram
Calories 262	Sugars .... 6 grams
Total Fat .... 13 grams	Protein .... 26 grams
Saturated Fat .... 3 grams	Sodium .... 112 milligrams
Calories from Fat 121	

BASIC BARBECUE SAUCE

12 servings/serving size: 2 Tbsp.

Use this version instead of bottled, and you will agree homemade has its benefits. Store in the freezer.

- 1 Tbsp. olive oil
- 1 medium onion, chopped
- 1-1/4 cups tomato sauce
- 1 bay leaf
- 1/4 tsp. curry powder

- Fresh ground pepper
- 1 Tbsp. white vinegar
- 1/4 tsp. dry mustard
- 1/4 tsp. hot pepper sauce
- 1 Tbsp. chopped parsley

1. In a medium saucepan, heat oil, and saute the onion until tender, about 5 minutes. Add the remaining ingredients, and simmer for 20 minutes.
2. Discard the bay leaf, and transfer sauce to a container.

Vegetable Exchange 1
Calories 24
Total Fat . . . . 1 gram
  Saturated Fat . . . . 0 grams
  Calories from Fat 11
Cholesterol . . . . 0 milligrams

Total Carbohydrate . . . . 3 grams
  Dietary Fiber . . . . 0 grams
  Sugars . . . . 2 grams
Protein . . . . 1 gram
Sodium . . . . 6 milligrams

TANGY MARINADE*

Makes 1-2/3 cups/use 1/3 cup per recipe

Great for marinating beef or pork before grilling. Store extra portions in the freezer.

- 1 cup unsweetened pineapple juice
- 1 garlic clove, minced
- 1/3 cup lite soy sauce

- 1 tsp. ground ginger
- 1/3 cup low-calorie Italian salad dressing

1. In a shallow dish, combine all ingredients; mixing thoroughly.
2. Keep refrigerated until ready to use.

Starch/Bread Exchange 1/2
Calories 44
Total Fat . . . . 0 grams
  Saturated Fat . . . . 0 grams
  Calories from Fat 0
Cholesterol . . . . 0 milligrams

Total Carbohydrate . . . . 9 grams
  Dietary Fiber . . . . 0 grams
  Sugars . . . . 9 grams
Protein . . . . 1 gram
Sodium . . . . 870 milligrams

* This recipe is high in sodium.

WESTERN OMELET

2 servings/serving size: 1/2 omelet

A good basic omelet recipe—experiment with your favorite vegetables.

- ◆ **1-1/2 tsp. canola oil**
- ◆ **3 egg substitute equivalents**
- ◆ **1/4 cup minced lean ham**
- ◆ **2 Tbsp. minced green pepper**
- ◆ **2 Tbsp. minced onion**
- ◆ **Dash salt**
- ◆ **Fresh ground pepper**

1. In a medium nonstick skillet over medium low heat, heat the oil.
2. In a small mixing bowl, beat eggs slightly, and add remaining ingredients. Pour egg mixture into heated skillet.
3. When omelet begins to set, gently lift the edges of omelet with a spatula, and tilt skillet to allow uncooked portion to flow underneath. Continue cooking until eggs are firm, then transfer to serving platter.

Lean Meat Exchange 2
Calories 96
Total Fat . . . . 4 grams
   Saturated Fat . . . . 1 gram
   Calories from Fat 39
Cholesterol . . . . 8 milligrams

Total Carbohydrate . . . . 3 grams
   Dietary Fiber . . . . 0 grams
   Sugars . . . . 2 grams
Protein . . . . 11 grams
Sodium . . . . 379 milligrams

BAKED FRENCH TOAST WITH RASPBERRY SAUCE*

4 servings/serving size: 2 slices

*H*ere is french toast that you soak overnight in a tasty batter and let puff up in the oven.

- ◆ 4 egg substitute equivalents
- ◆ 2/3 cup skim milk
- ◆ 1 tsp. maple extract
- ◆ 1 tsp. cinnamon
- ◆ 1/2 tsp. nutmeg
- ◆ 8 slices whole-wheat bread

- ◆ 2 cups frozen or fresh raspberries
- ◆ 1 Tbsp. orange juice
- ◆ 1 tsp. vanilla extract
- ◆ 2 tsp. cornstarch

1. Beat together eggs, milk, maple extract, cinnamon, and nutmeg in a medium bowl.
2. In a casserole dish, lay bread slices side by side. Pour over the egg-milk mixture, cover, and place in refrigerator overnight.
3. The next day, bake the french toast at 350 degrees for 30 minutes until golden brown and slightly puffed.
4. To make raspberry sauce, puree raspberries in a blender. Strain to remove seeds. In a small saucepan, combine pureed berries with orange juice, vanilla, and cornstarch. Bring to a boil, and cook for 1 minute until mixture is thickened. Serve over french toast.

....

Starch/Bread Exchange	2-1/2	Total Carbohydrate	38 grams
Calories	216	Dietary Fiber	8 grams
Total Fat	3 grams	Sugars	8 grams
Saturated Fat	1 gram	Protein	12 grams
Calories from Fat	25	Sodium	400 milligrams
Cholesterol	1 milligram		

* This recipe is relatively high in sodium.

BLUEBERRY SCONES

8 servings/serving size: 1 3-inch scone

*T*ypical store-bought scones have a lot more fat and calories than these.

- 1/2 cup buttermilk at room temperature
- 3/4 cup orange juice
- Grated peel of one orange
- 2-1/4 cups whole-wheat pastry flour or unbleached white flour
- 1 tsp. baking soda
- 1 tsp. cream of tartar
- 3 Tbsp. fructose
- 2 Tbsp. low-calorie margarine, cold
- 1 cup fresh or frozen (thawed) blueberries

1. In a small bowl, combine buttermilk, orange juice, and orange peel. Set aside.
2. Sift together flour, baking soda, cream of tartar, and fructose into a large bowl. Using a fork or pastry blender, cut in the margarine until well combined. Stir in buttermilk mixture and blueberries, and mix gently by hand until well combined.
3. Turn batter onto a lightly floured cookie sheet, and pat into a circle about 3/4-inch thick and 8 inches across. Use a sharp knife to cut the circle into eight wedges, cutting almost all the way through. Place pan in a preheated 375-degree oven, and bake for 25 minutes until lightly browned.

....

Starch/Bread Exchange	2	Total Carbohydrate	33 grams
Calories	168	Dietary Fiber	5 grams
Total Fat	2 grams	Sugars	9 grams
Saturated Fat	0 grams	Protein	5 grams
Calories from Fat	20	Sodium	144 milligrams
Cholesterol	1 milligram		

PINEAPPLE MUFFINS

1 dozen/serving size: 1 muffin

A welcomed addition to the breakfast table. Just add fruit or juice and yogurt.

- 1-1/2 cups whole-wheat flour or pastry flour
- 2 tsp. baking powder
- 1/2 tsp. baking soda
- 1/4 cup fructose
- 2 tsp. cinnamon
- 2 egg substitute equivalents
- 2/3 cup unsweetened applesauce
- 1 cup crushed canned pineapple, drained
- 1/2 cup diced dried apricots

1. In a medium bowl, combine dry ingredients.
2. In a large bowl, combine remaining ingredients. Slowly add dry ingredients to wet ingredients, and mix until blended. Do not beat.
3. Place batter into prepared muffin cups, filling 2/3 full.
4. Bake at 350 degrees for 25 minutes until golden brown.

Starch/Bread Exchange	1	Cholesterol	0 milligrams
Fruit Exchange	1/2	Total Carbohydrate	21 grams
Calories	95	Dietary Fiber	3 grams
Total Fat	0 grams	Sugars	9 grams
Saturated Fat	0 grams	Protein	3 grams
Calories from Fat	0	Sodium	101 milligrams

FRESH BLUEBERRY PANCAKES

8 servings/serving size: 2 4- to 5-inch pancakes

*W*hat's breakfast without a stack of warm blueberry pancakes?

- ◆ 1 cup flour
- ◆ 1/2 tsp. baking soda
- ◆ 1-1/2 tsp. baking powder
- ◆ 1 egg substitute equivalent
- ◆ 1 cup low-fat buttermilk

- ◆ 1 Tbsp. canola oil
- ◆ 1/2 cup fresh blueberries, washed and drained
- ◆ Nonstick cooking spray

1. Combine dry ingredients together in a medium-sized bowl and set aside.
2. In a small bowl, combine egg, buttermilk, and oil, and mix well. Add mixture to the dry ingredients, stirring until moistened, then gently fold in the blueberries.
3. Coat a griddle or skillet with cooking spray. Pour 2 Tbsp. of batter for each pancake onto hot griddle. Turn the pancakes when tops are covered with tiny bubbles and edges are golden brown.

....

Starch/Bread Exchange 1	Cholesterol . . . . 1 milligram
Fat Exchange 1/2	Total Carbohydrate . . . . 15 grams
Calories 94	Dietary Fiber . . . . 1 gram
Total Fat . . . . 2 grams	Sugars . . . . 3 grams
Saturated Fat . . . . 0 grams	Protein . . . . 3 grams
Calories from Fat 20	Sodium . . . . 153 milligrams

TURKEY SAUSAGE PATTIES

4 servings/serving size: about 2 oz.

*P*repare one day in advance, and the flavor will be even better.

- 1/2 lb. ground turkey
- 1/4 cup low-sodium beef broth
- 1/2 Tbsp. lemon juice
- 2 Tbsp. fine dried bread crumbs
- 1/8 tsp. fennel seeds

- 1/8 tsp. ground ginger
- 1/2 tsp. grated lemon peel
- 1/4 tsp. fresh minced sage
- Fresh ground pepper
- 1/8 tsp. ground red pepper
- Nonstick cooking spray

1. In a large bowl, combine all ingredients except cooking spray; cover and set aside for at least 15 to 20 minutes (refrigerate if overnight). Coat a large skillet with cooking spray, and place over medium heat until hot.
2. Shape mixture into 4 patties, and place in hot skillet. Fry patties for 5 to 6 minutes on each side, remove, and let drain on paper towels. Transfer to serving platter, and serve while hot.

••

Lean Meat Exchange	2	Total Carbohydrate	3 grams
Calories	113	Dietary Fiber	0 grams
Total Fat	6 grams	Sugars	0 grams
Saturated Fat	2 grams	Protein	11 grams
Calories from Fat	55	Sodium	69 milligrams
Cholesterol	30 milligrams		

HASH BROWNS

4 servings/serving size: 1/2 cup

*L*ove hash browns, but not the fat content? Don't worry with these greaseless, yet tasty, potatoes.

- ◆ **2 large baking potatoes (about 10 oz. each)**
- ◆ **2 Tbsp. minced onion**
- ◆ **1 tsp. garlic powder**
- ◆ **1/2 tsp. dried thyme**
- ◆ **Fresh ground pepper**
- ◆ **Nonstick cooking spray**

1. Peel and shred each potato with a hand grater or a food processor with grater attachment. Combine potatoes with onion and spices.
2. Coat a large skillet with cooking spray, and place over medium heat until hot.
3. Pack potato mixture firmly into skillet; cook mixture for 6–8 minutes or until bottom is browned. Invert potato patty onto a plate and return to the skillet, cooked side up.
4. Continue cooking over medium heat for another 6–8 minutes until bottom is browned. Remove from heat and cut into 4 wedges.

....

Starch/Bread Exchange 1-1/2
Calories 100
Total Fat .... 0 grams
   Saturated Fat .... 0 grams
   Calories from Fat 0
Cholesterol .... 0 milligrams

Total Carbohydrate .... 23 grams
   Dietary Fiber .... 2 grams
   Sugars .... 2 grams
Protein .... 2 grams
Sodium .... 2 grams

CORN CAKES

6 servings/serving size: 2 4-inch cakes

These are not only good for breakfast, but for a light dinner too.

- ◆ 2/3 cup unbleached white flour
- ◆ 1/3 cup whole-wheat flour or pastry flour
- ◆ 2 tsp. baking powder
- ◆ 1 Tbsp. fructose
- ◆ 3/4 cup buttermilk
- ◆ 1 egg substitute equivalent
- ◆ 2 Tbsp. canola oil
- ◆ 1 cup corn kernels (frozen or fresh; if frozen, defrost)

1. Combine all dry ingredients in a medium bowl.
2. In another bowl, combine buttermilk, egg, and oil. Stir in corn kernels. Slowly add this mixture to dry ingredients, just to blend. A few lumps will remain.
3. On a heated nonstick griddle, pour 1/4 cup batter per cake. Cook cakes for about 3 minutes, flip them over, and cook 1 to 2 minutes more, until golden brown. Serve.

....

Starch/Bread Exchange 1-1/2	Cholesterol .... 1 milligram
Fat Exchange 1	Total Carbohydrate .... 24 grams
Calories 161	Dietary Fiber .... 2 grams
Total Fat .... 5 grams	Sugars .... 4 grams
Saturated Fat .... 1 gram	Protein .... 5 grams
Calories from Fat 47	Sodium .... 151 milligrams

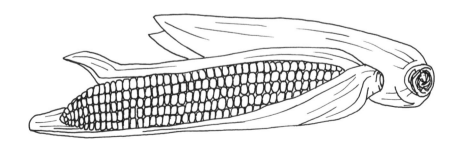

COUNTRY CEREAL

6 servings/serving size: 1/2 cup

Instead of the usual cold cereal, try this fiber-rich cereal dotted with raisins.

- **2 cups skim milk**
- **1/2 cup raisins**
- **1 tsp. cinnamon**
- **3 cups precooked brown rice**

- **2 strawberry halves per serving**
- **1-1/2 tsp. pure maple syrup per serving**

1. In a medium saucepan over medium heat, combine milk, rice, raisins, and cinnamon. Bring mixture to a boil, stirring occasionally. Reduce heat; cover and simmer for 8 to 10 minutes or until mixture thickens.
2. Spoon cereal into bowls, top with strawberries and syrup and serve.

....

Starch/Bread Exchange 2	Cholesterol . . . . 1 milligram
Fruit Exchange 1	Total Carbohydrate . . . . 44 grams
Calories 206	Dietary Fiber . . . . 3 grams
Total Fat . . . . 1 gram	Sugars . . . . 20 grams
Saturated Fat . . . . 0 grams	Protein . . . . 6 grams
Calories from Fat 11	Sodium . . . . 50 milligrams

INDEX

DIG INTO OUR *RECIPE-PACKED PANTRY OF COOKBOOKS AND MENU PLANNERS*

Healthy Selects: Spark Plugs for Your Taste Buds

Dozens of recipes were chosen for each *Healthy Selects* cookbook, but only the 60 most tempting were chosen. Every recipe will fit nicely into your healthy meal plan. Calories, fats, sodium, carbohydrates, cholesterol counts, and food exchanges accompany every recipe.

◆ GREAT STARTS & FINE FINISHES

Now you can begin every dinner with an enticing appetizer and finish it off with a "now I'm REALLY satisfied" dessert. Choose from recipes like Crab-Filled Mushrooms, Broiled Shrimp with Garlic, Baked Scallops, Creamy Tarragon Dip, or Cheesy Tortilla Wedges to start; serve Cherry Cobbler, Fresh Apple Pie, Cherry Cheesecake, Chocolate Cupcakes, or dozens of others to finish. Softcover. #CCBGSFF
Nonmember: $8.95/Member: $7.15

◆ EASY & ELEGANT ENTREES

Tired of leaving the dinner table feeling like you've had nothing more than a snack? Pull up a chair to *Easy & Elegant Entrees*. Now you can sit down to Fettucine with Peppers and Broccoli, Steak with Brandied Onions, Shrimp Creole, and dozens of others. They taste like they took hours to prepare, but you can put them on the table in minutes. Softcover. #CCBEEE
Nonmember: $8.95/Member: $7.15

◆ SAVORY SOUPS & SALADS

When your meals need a little something extra, or you just want something light, invite *Savory Soups & Salads* to lunch and dinner. They just might become your favorite guests. Choose from Pasta-Stuffed Tomato Salad, Mediterranean Chicken Salad, Hot Clam Chowder, Cool Gazpacho, and more. Softcover. #CCBSSS
Nonmember: $8.95/Member: $7.15

◆ QUICK & HEARTY MAIN DISHES

Softcover. #CCBQHMD. *Nonmember: $8.95/Member: $7.15*

◆ SIMPLE & TASTY SIDE DISHES

Add a spark of flavor to your main course from four tasty categories of easy-to-prepare sides. In just minutes you can have Herb-Broiled Tomatoes, Sherried Peppers with Bean Sprouts, Brown Rice with Mushrooms, Zucchini & Carrot Salad, Scalloped Potatoes, and dozens of others keeping company with your favorite entrees. Softcover. #CCBSTSD
Nonmember: $8.95/Member: $7.15

The *Month of Meals* series:
Automatic meal planning with a turn of the page

Each *Month of Meals* menu planner offers 28 days' worth of fresh new menu choices. The pages are split into thirds and interchangeable, so you can flip to any combination of breakfast, lunch, and dinner. So no matter which combinations you choose, your nutrients and exchanges will still be correct for the entire day—automatically!

♦ **MONTH OF MEALS**

Choose from Chicken Cacciatore, Oven Fried Fish, Sloppy Joes, Crab Cakes, many others. Spiral-bound. #CMPMOM
Nonmember: $12.50/Member: $9.95

♦ **MONTH OF MEALS 2**

Month of Meals 2 features tips and meal suggestions for Mexican, Italian, and Chinese restaurants. Menu choices include Beef Burritos, Chop Suey, Veal Piccata, Stuffed Peppers, many others. Spiral-bound. #CMPMOM2
Nonmember: $12.50/Member: $9.95

♦ **MONTH OF MEALS 3**

How long has it been since you could eat fast food without guilt? Now you can—*Month of Meals 3* shows you how. Choose from McDonald's, Wendy's, Taco Bell, and others. Menu choices include Kentucky Fried Chicken, Stouffer's Macaroni and Cheese, Fajita in a Pita, Seafood Stir-Fry, others. Spiral-bound. #CMPMOM3
Nonmember: $12.50/Member: $9.95

♦ **MONTH OF MEALS 4**

Beef up your meal planning with our "meat and potatoes" menu planner. Menu options include Oven Crispy Chicken, Beef Stroganoff, Cornbread Pie, many others. Spiral-bound. #CMPMOM4
Nonmember: $12.50/Member: $9.95

♦ **MONTH OF MEALS 5**

Automatic meal planning goes vegetarian! Choose from a garden of fresh selections like Eggplant Italian, Stuffed Zucchini, Cucumbers with Dill Dressing, Vegetable Lasagna, many others. Spiral-bound. #CMPMOM5
Nonmember: $12.50/Member: $9.95

♦ **HEALTHY HOMESTYLE COOKBOOK**

Choose from more than 150 healthy new recipes with old-fashioned great taste. Just like grandma used to make—but **without** all that fat. Complete nutrition information—calories, protein, fat, fiber, saturated fat, sodium, cholesterol, carbohydrate counts, and diabetic exchanges—accompanies every recipe. Special introductory section features "how-to" cooking tips, plus energy- and time-saving tips for microwaving. Lay-flat binding allows hands-free reference to any recipe. Softcover. #CCBHHS
Nonmember: $12.50/Member: $9.95

☐ **YES!** Please send me the following books:

Book Name: _____
Item Number: _____ Quantity: _____
Price Each: _____ Total: _____

Book Name: _____
Item Number: _____ Quantity: _____
Price Each: _____ Total: _____

Book Name: _____
Item Number: _____ Quantity: _____
Price Each: _____ Total: _____

Book Name: _____
Item Number: _____ Quantity: _____
Price Each: _____ Total: _____

Publications Subtotal $ _____
Virginia residents add 4.5% state sales tax $ _____
Add shipping & handling (see chart) $ _____
Add $15 for each international shipment $ _____
GRAND TOTAL $ _____

Name _____
Address _____
City/State/Zip _____

☐ Payment enclosed (check or money order)
☐ Charge my: ☐ VISA ☐ MasterCard ☐ American Express

Account Number _____
Signature _____
Exp. Date _____   CHA95HS

Shipping & Handling
Up to $30 . . . . .add $3.00
$30.01-$50 . . . . .add $4.00
Over $50 . . . . .add 8%

Mail to: American Diabetes Association
          1970 Chain Bridge Road
          McLean, VA 22109-0592

Allow 2-3 weeks for shipment. Add $3 for each extra shipping address. Prices subject to change without notice. Foreign orders must be paid in U.S. funds, drawn on a U.S. bank.